A Dedicat

Maeve McKenna

First published February 2022 by Fly on the Wall Press
Published in the UK by
Fly on the Wall Press
56 High Lea Rd
New Mills
Derbyshire
SK22 3DP

www.flyonthewallpress.co.uk
ISBN: 978-1-913211-73-8
EBOOK: 978-1-913211-74-5
Copyright Maeve McKenna © 2022

The right of Maeve McKenna to be identified as the author of this work has been asserted in accordance with the Copyright, Designs and Patents Act 1988.

Typesetting by Isabelle Kenyon. Cover photo Unsplash, edited by Joel Williams.

All rights reserved. No part of this publication may be reproduced, stored in or introduced into a retrieval system, or transmitted in any form, or by any means (electronic, mechanical, photocopying, recording or otherwise) without prior written permissions of the publisher. Any person who does any unauthorised act in relation to this publication may be liable for criminal prosecution and civil claims for damages.

A CIP Catalogue record for this book is available from the British Library.

For S,O,S and K

Contents

The Sound Of Distance	4
A Dedication To Drowning	6
Holy Pleasure	8
A Recipe For Hunger	9
Propagation	10
Mute Marriage	12
Dredge	14
Family Web	15
A Burial In The Home	16
Never Tell Your Business	17
Cat Mirror	18
Waking Is November	19
Dancing Is Deadly	20
A Meal For One	22
Undelivered	23
Fertile	24
Carriage	25
Shadow Waiting	26
Cat Without Claws	27
Performance	28
Cooled Boiled Water	29
Gerard's	30
Tent	31
Knitting Wounds	32
Bookmarker	33

The Sound Of Distance

Your son is trying to kill you.
He's thinking about it and you know this.
You suggest a walk on the beach,
idle water, the distraction of sand dunes,
and wind; the need for words lost
to it when speech was still forming.

He's been in his room. For months,
you say, but it's fifteen years really. You make
pasta he has to navigate so you can
watch him twist a fork around the loose bits,
sometimes sucking the dangling threads
of food into his mouth as he inhales —
one eye on you — and it vanishes into the
slurping silence of another meal time.

You say, *isn't this nice*,
and it is, the moment of him eating:
his jaw line jutting through pale skin,
fingers tapping, throat flexing,
and without realising, his chewing
becomes all the noise you can hope for.

A little boy, all pudgy shivering, togs falling
off the crease of his bum, sand between his
floppy toes, feet in your hands rubbing
them warm, smiles sitting in the back
of the car, just the two of you —
his favourite blanket, your fussing. Oh,
the weightless quiet.

The thud you hear after you hear it,
lives in rear mirrors, too late to react
when a deer propels itself into headlights.
Each time you plummet
into the depth of your child,
birthday cards unopened.

A Dedication To Drowning

Stretched like a drum
a coating of me covers
my skeletal frame.
For now, I am crouched
at the shoreline, the night
grips, my back a fist.

Out past the cut of land and sea —
where everything
was once you and nothing
was me —
a kind of balance prevails.
Not here, though. Not among
the creeping pull lapping
at my toes, luring me back
inside the silence of water,
the idle current a mouth
full of promises, echoing closer.

Now, I can't trust my feet,
they are traitors, like my mind,
like your face.

Sand is under everywhere you are not
as I think of you then, swimming to shore,
your wide shoulders an Orca's
tail slicing the surface,
your head rising through
the ripples.

You asked me once why I never swim.
I told you, *drowning*
twice takes dedication.

Holy Pleasure

In unison, I watch us leave as we enter the communion,
your toe-tongue mastery of crumpling a hot, ironed sheet,

my handy work undone, and I, grateful for it. This time,
you plump the pillow exactly at the right angle.

My head, flailing for years, now the stunned stillness
of a shop-window mannequin. What followed I can't name,

but do recall the dogs hackled back for most of that night.
When morning cajoled across our bare shoulders,

I was, well, relieved to find you arriving, all contrite
and sweating, unlike before when your guilty descent

concocted another ascension, hands imitating Christ,
you risen that we may never sin this low alone, or,

with the folly of faithless youth, tip our lapping lips
to a waiting mouth, its sour breath a forgiving hymn

we have hummed to incessantly.

A Recipe For Hunger

Hungry, our eyes point, aim where hurt is willing.
Reactions simmer on the cooker ring
until boiling; a pot for us to stare blindly into.

I make meals from the taste of my own voice: sickly
sweet sauce infused with alcohol-marinated lemon rind.

Crumbs gather like demons
on a chopping board. On the dinner plate, slivers
of dissected flesh mangle around a fork's teeth,

then the massive feasting of strangers in exodus.
We keep returning. Riots! Sucking sounds against bone,
meat left to marinate overnight under fingernails, knives

and tumblers streaking. After supper, stunned
by the stench of boots kicked off at the low point

of a sprung base, soon after by the nightmare-infested
fist of a child at 4am. I'm preparing to tell you this:

each day is birth, and a burial.
Until, at the blindside of the bed, the smell of leather
cooking something exotic.

Propagation

They cluster inside spread-eagled legs,
hands bony
wings, faces pleading,

hinged

on palms. I know them,
these people, their
atrocious need,

soured

breath of last night's lust.
Still willing in the morning,
I relent for a puce

cheek,

uprooted pubic hair. Or,
occasional understanding.
I adore the life in them,

more

than mine; chiselled
from marrow, a blood-infused
platelet, how they dine to fill

bellies

on propagation. Oh! hero.
Oh! Lover. Oh, desire
from consequence —

unwill me.

Mute Marriage

The slight discomfort we compare
to warm rain; the excitement

when tinged by it, until coats
stiffen & smell.

Faint shock dimples
your cheeks, discovering

hearts deform because
of a callousness in us.

You haven't been listening,
My Love. Thoughts fester

because of them. I can't locate
our voices; talk of futures,

scattering pasts here
and where. Unopened

tube of confetti on the back
seat the morning after.

At the retail park, I am treading
tarmac with the Water God

who has churched me,
waiting for my life to be over,

or forgiven. I call you because
a tyre is flat. I want to admit

winter is cruelly in us, blessings
are a curse, rooks know our plans.

I live in dread most days
of the low-set alloys

our youngest son careens
the back roads on. *I couldn't bear*

to lose his life, I say,
and wait years to hear it.

Dredge

I allow one thought to drown my current idolisation of this walking to and beyond the debris of the shoreline; mutilated crabs upturned, bloated stomach's hardening under a rigid winter sun, guts thin trails snared in shrivelled seaweed, several dismembered pincers crusting some feet away, dusty sea-salt coating the edges of my lips and I lick, lick, suck hard until bitter grit softens under my tongue and I am alert again to its impurities, intent on pushing forward past the line of washed-up shells, many shattered by my pacing back and forth, and further, on the unrelenting horizon, seagulls speckle a trawler's mast I think I can swim to, I think.

Family Web

A spider where you point your gaze:
brothers, tidied for battle, pinned
unarmed to the floor, ready for the killing

in them to reveal itself, not yet hard in their ways.
It will come. Your sisters are younger,
unknowing of the consequences of growing —

the absolution needed to harbour death.
The room spins, creatures scurry
under dust particles in corners,

leather strap stroked for the prettiest child.
You know fear. The boys will too.
Your sisters keep reaching to the highest wall for it.

A Burial In The Home

The dog is dead. Now, house flies
are dive-bombing into coffins of fine lace.
Grinning mask inside a cardboard box.

Forgotten lovers appear as clouds.
Today, somewhere, a face is smiling.
The sea is an acquaintance

which returns friendship as a swelling corpse.
Your hands lower the body —
not as we remember it — ankle-deep.

I have yet to begin looking down.

At the back door, wind. Soon, to regale us,
more wind. The insects are rampant. A troop
of magpies sift soil with meticulous claws.

It is said only three people in your life
understand you.
Today, tomorrow's deaths have begun.

Never Tell Your Business

We never talked about the noise; family crashing
inside a family and outside, silent families. I have only

this: my mother hung worn rugs and five bodies
from the clothesline, thin shapes flapping with fear, damp

with love, slapped legs and a belt around the ears —
never tell your business. Mornings, when the whole house

was asleep, I cuddled the dog, mimicked the budgie's
attempts to fly. I never took the dog

for walks: some dreams weren't mine. Today, I imagine this
as poetry in my poems. You see, we didn't dare be anything.

Instead, I boiled the kettle, careful not to scald myself, stirred
the overnight porridge or chicken casserole with a finger,

took milk bottles in from the front step before they soured
under the summer sun. In winter, frost separated the cream,

I can't forget this. I cleaned whatever my brothers left
on the chopping board, lined-up shoes, never opened the curtains.

Once, creeping out to the back garden, terrified I would wake
them with my fumbling at the rusted latch, the whining

hinges, the yelping dog, I imagined leaving. No one heard.
Also, around that time, I was told I was a quiet girl.

Cat Mirror

They clung to walls in places we called home,
plotted revenge, like the claws of that feral
we tamed with scraps of food
and a newspaper bed. Shards we could
never piece back together, bodies unfolding
inside coats hung in halls, the fickle latch
of fatherless homecomings
as the evening sun settled over other houses.

The slap of morning water smeared itself
across our attempted childhood
and each sunrise her smile froze;
compacted glass face glistening in a handbag,
beside her lipstick, in the follicles of a hairbrush.

Once, she invested in a life size mirror.
We crawled about, contorted, watching our bodies
be other animals; all rickety bone, matted hair
and little else, while she flounced under
the reflective plume of a French cigarette, cradling
the cat like a new fur coat, in the pose
of a dinner-dance goddess.

Waking Is November

The weight of waking — compounded
memory — an inheritance of empty vodka bottles

and your favourite faux-fur coat. One unframed
wedding photo. An empty ashtray. Beneath the bed, inside

the zipped pocket of a handbag, rolls of twenty-pound notes
tied with elastic. There, too, folded neatly between

the blank pages of a bank deposit book in your maiden name,
two handwritten letters; replies

to an advert in the personal classifieds.
Night is living hours away and it's November again.

Dancing Is Deadly

In the beginning, when everything was possible,
when events of high gravity revealed
our low parts,
we were always last to leave the party.

Hallways strewn with lager cans
and turpentine bodies — mesmerising graveyards
of beautiful bonfires — it seemed to play death
was a youthful gamble we rolled dice at.

On the white sterile sheet, they discount fingers
and toes, eyes colourful and bleak;
like ball-pits in a disused play centre.
A radio plays out a 90's classic, fingernails tapping

on chrome rails to the waltz of a medicine trolley,
rhythmic woman naked from the waist down,
raucous revellers congregating at red pools
where an infant would ta-da from; floppy limbed,

wobbly with music — our favourite song.
The fist-rolled newspaper,
flattened and saved
in a shoe box with mittens and a lock of hair

plucked from under a fully formed bonnet,
the poorly-designed gown
and brand new fluffy slippers, after,
made dancing difficult.

A Meal For One

Let's call the bowl a peace offering: *I bring you
this sorry weight.* A final resting place,
almost flawless in design, smooth edges, sterile
surface where a cracked egg settles, perfectly
formed as it sways on a hospital trolley, whipped out,
lapping at the cold touch, floppy, like raspberry jelly

infused with pomegranate; the last supper.
Wheels spin through corridors, flicking
back and forward, turning on themselves,
never changing direction. A man
in blue, hairnet clogs, checking his watch,
clock-off time, his retreat to normal life

catapulting this new time beyond
the bedside locker onto your bruised lap.
Think of a woman in stirrups, belly flat,
hope heavy, insides abandoned,
the hunger of the unbloody.

My Mother said if you have eggs
in the fridge, you have a meal.
She had five children.

Undelivered

Today is culling day for the undelivered;
vacuum cupping a hairless skull.

I feel you exiting my groin, bit by bit.
Bundles of puce membrane flop out over entrails,

squeezing lungs through brittle ribcages too shallow
to bear breath, too soon to un-mother you.

Was your face veiled, belly tethered,
your cry un-slapped? You are only questions.

If I could hold you, coax your chest open, blood-fill
each pulse-less chamber, lay it plump as a pillow

under mine, I would. Not within flattened flesh will I mend
you; fuse fontanels, salvage from a bucket your limbs,

knit sinew to bone, make you intact as you began,
offer your fractured heart the empty whole of mine.

Fertile

I am the womb behind the wolf's ribcage,
its fertile scent sifting through the pack,
the stench of bloodied meat at arousal
as teeth fondle matted mane.

I am the hunger of the mob, ageless,
fur preened by night goons that pepper
the coal black woods, silhouettes ignited
by shooting stars, eyes darting, lined and shadowed.

Here, mother dogs discard their thinning hair-coats,
drool tongues, flaunt flesh
as if in heat, the egg sack still spouting
blood, month after month.

I am the future breed, hunted by the past,
bludgeoned by barren paths, a death-fog languishing
on my breath. And, on the river floor, a cub, limp
beneath stones in a plastic shopping bag.

Carriage

The train station has a high wall and bedding plants
clinging to the incline. On the platform, two men stand

far apart. I am going nowhere, visiting the station at 5:45am
in March, nearly late for the train I haven't booked;

for the flower show, which is to be bright
as it is at the bottom of a cared-for garden.

Fog has yet to release the bank. I am sure flowers are there.
Frost battles a rise in my body-heat but I am happy.

Headlights are injections under the bridge.
Both men board, one steps back, the other nods,

as strangers do, knowing the strangeness in others.
A woman wobbles onto the train, appears to be sweating,

I see her fussing, unzipping her coat, as you do
visiting somewhere, unsure if you are welcome.

This tunnel out. I wish them safe exit.
My hand rises to wave. I want to say, *stop!* The whistle goes.

After, when the wind catches up with the last carriage,
I am the other side of the track, dead-heading daisies.

Shadow Waiting

in memory of Mother and Baby homes

It's always November, always 5am and you lie rigid
in a cooling sweat, dawn yet to reach under the bolted door.

Some hours earlier you sat rocking at your bedsit window.
A couple, arm in arm, cavort under shafts of orange;

the distant shadows of love are unbearable. You are folding
a sheet, tracing the edges with aging fingertips

back and forth along each crease. You do this most nights.
Others you spend polishing a brass flower vase.

The thump of boots on the stairs propels you under the bed
where you remain with the sin of unworn, leather shoes.

In the forgiveness of morning you lean in, sit watching mothers
walk away from their children, unsure if they blow a kiss.

The day congregates around you in silence, until once again,
black noise descends, then separates, revealing faces, names,
screams.

It's forty years since you were spared the shaved scalp,
holy linen, bunches of rosary beads as improvised fists, your baby.

Forty more years, waiting for them to come for you.

Cat Without Claws

The body ticks its skeletal tock along skin: armoury
matted, greying in places. Time-scabbed flesh
protrudes over potions. A thinning lip smudges
claret onto the filter tip of a barbed wire cigarette.

She was adored once; a noisy mechanical
toy and gourmet food portions in petite pouches
for her first Christmas. A diamante collar
followed the next year. Then, the tom arrived.

Wretched side-streets became home, an endless colony of fur
flouncing behind, the stooped decline reversed
in a series of doorways - respite from the hissing years.
Then, the tom returned.

Late in life she reappeared, a burden heavy in the forgiveness
of things, and I, without shame, salvaged
the dazzling collar from a box in the attic and punctured
a new hole for her emaciated neck.

Performance

Wounded urine, yellow-bruised and pungent
with an assault of red in the bowl. Wait! The animals

exist to devour their bodies and you make tasting
yours a constant dying. You are guzzling

fluids like a drought is cracking lines
across your face. Fickle skin, itchy and tight, fingers

can't warm there now. But, oh! The latent tingle!
Even the flesh funnel and its thirst

dried up during those rare, sultry summers. Then,
the makeshift wet. You came, unbalanced, legs trembling

on a circus wire, pounding applause inside our skin hovel.
A ritual of one, years scampering

over lust-moist sheets, cold edges where we
retreat. This is performance, persistent

and loud, a tribute to self. And the baby, now a man,
still clapping inside the audience of a woman.

Cooled Boiled Water

I am trying to bend a mind.

Can I imagine the moon as a suffocating balloon,
ready to inhale, siphoning lungs from the earth —
which is a cardboard box of discarded toys,
metal and plastic? Or stars, the eyes of a wolf-pack,
in the dark world forest,

glaring behind spindly trees —
which are needles in a pin cushion. Just that.
Or rivers as paths guzzling swamped ground,
drowning the carcasses of roads that lead home —

which is a state of familiarity only.
Or bodies as a surface to sketch new ways,
tracing escape routes through veins —
which are tracks of blood —

which are cooled boiled water
dredging metal and plastic from a cardboard box,
while starry eyes take aim with spindly pins
and puncture flesh,

and the river path devours familiarity,
and sketches are cuts on a skin map
bleeding cooled, boiled, water.

Gerard's

under a rubbish truck Gerard's hanging from the second-floor balcony syringes stuck to chewing gum on the chalked stones below Gerard's face reversed in the wing-mirror of a debt-paid Yamaha 125 falling like his mother's wedding ring into the pawn-shop falling with no feeling of loss as his shin-bone punctures the ulcerated crater of pus the bulging mass on Gerard's acned forehead dangling over his gouged nose-lining his sniffling mid-facial erosion Gerard's head hitting the continuous white line smack but no smack a mob of grey and white gulls with fluorescent orange beaks like couriers arriving with party pizzas circling the scene with winged antenna city radars for guts Gerard's bottom lip split and two front teeth vanished into the swollen red collision of flesh Gerard, who French-kissed so good with those lips who said *come here come on please* Gerard who held my hand on that first trip to the gurrier soul who stole words of violence from our alley mouths made them accents of peace for a night Gerard's finger severed by that gold wedding ring Gerard who worked had a pay check on Fridays Gerard who didn't smoke cigarettes there a heap on the road in bits under the exhaust finger twitching over at the dried-out manhole Gerard's father wheeling the rims of a motorbike home months later after the hospital, after the debt came back from the wheelie-bin ghost-boys behind the Jervis Shopping Centre Gerard in recovery on a frame Gerard gone again Gerard in cable-ties Gerard revving his body into the ground leg missing finger too Gerard's gorgeous grey lips and the yellow bulb over his blue smile Gerard nailing *happy-dying-face* Gerard's bandaged wrists punctured forearms pinhole tracks Gerard's tattoos his lovely Granny dead in blurry ink on his arm Gerard's Ma there too

Tent

From the pocket radio, black magic swirls,
air does too, then thickens —
as if anything could get any darker.

I've known you three hours and thirty-four minutes.
You fidget at necking whisky, take too long
rolling a joint, seem kind.

When the daddy-long-legs buries landmines
under the duffle-coat blanket, I still tip-toe
in, not revealing my fear of hearts living

with wings, unreasonable to mention
in a field hooded by white fumes —
pretend angels we shelter under. Cellos sift

from the shore, bloated pet-names swept
in on hissing sea salt, strings snared
in seaweed on the fingerboard — some sounds

are too beautifully wooden. Earth shadows,
we form a lunar eclipse with each body heave, thrust
into the cold ground; two spirits we leave there.

Knitting Wounds

I want to say, carry on — to every injury.
They are temporary knots:

sensory loop of unhealing.
But look closer: as they knit, each hurt

is a duet of needles composing a scar.
They clack, clack, weave like dream-patterns

at 4am, but in time its harmony's purl,
each wound immersed

in lyrical machines of tone: kind voices.
At their busiest point thumbs

don't puncture: this is self-care. Contracted
as skin is by each penetrating

stitch, it is bodies of texture constructing
a flesh cardigan from wool.

Bookmarker

I knew its cost, heaving form agitated
on the shelf, the weight, how it would buckle
me. Not its thin story, or desperate
paragraphs that seeped close to the edges
of a blunt force ascent into oblivion,
or even the perfectly contagious sleekness
of its cover in my hands. No. None of this.

Not the aloofness of capitals, front cover
a boarded-up house in silhouette, wrought
iron gates padlocked, the infant woman
shoeless, fleeing. No. None of this nonsense.

There is so much pain I yearn for.
Paper cuts gather as a sequence of blades
slicing against my thumb, eyes magnified,
scanning each fitful page. I match words
with voices of panic, counsel truth in self truth,
nurse each sound into obscurity, wait
for it to heal, then hurt. Is it by this hearts

un-break the more numbness invades us?
Let's assemble our bodies, limb to limb against
the walls of unoccupied margins, hope pointed
like the scope of a firing squad, every cry
of submission as bullet hits bone; a reason
for applause. I am writing it for you. For me.

Acknowledgements

Thanks are due to the editors of the following publications in which some of these poems, or versions of them, have previously appeared: *Sand Magazine*, *The Blue Nib*, *Impspired*, *Skylight 47*, *Atrium*, *Black Bough Poetry*, *Bloody Amazing Anthology*, *Orbis*, *One Hand Clapping*, *MadSwirl*, *Boyne Berries*. *Sonder Magazine*, *The Poetry Bus 10th Anniversary Edition*. .

I have been blessed on my writing journey to meet and become friends with many writers. Without these wonderfully talented and kind people it would have been a lonely path. Writer and Poet Tess Gallagher for her friendship; my friend and poet Audrey Molly, for her encouragement and editorials, along with friends Morag Anderson, Barbara DeCoursey Roy, all of whom I met at Kevin Higgins' inspiring Over The Edge Workshops. Claire Loader, KT Slattery, Anne Walsh Donnelly, Bobbie Sparrow, members of a weekly prompt/feedback group where some of these poems emerged and were knocked into shape. Sinead McClure for urging me on with sound advice, Louise G. Cole for always listening; Gerard Beirne for giving me the confidence to enter the writing world and Anne Tannam for helping me find a belief in myself.

And finally, without his level head, constant wind-ups, his willing me on and rarely reading my poems, Kevin, I told you I'd do it, here goes — without you this wouldn't be possible. I love you. x

Author Biography

Maeve McKenna lives in rural Sligo, Ireland. In 2018, her work was shortlisted for the Red Line and highly commended in the iYeats International Poetry Competitions.

In 2019, she was highly commended in the Frances Ledwidge and longlisted in the Over The Edge Poetry competitions. She was joint runner-up in the Trim Poetry Competition and the Hanna Greally Poetry Competition, 2020.

Her work has been published in Mslexia, Orbis, Sand, The Galway Review, Marble Poetry, Channel Magazine, Fly on the Wall, The Haibun Journal, Bloody Amazing Anthology and Culture Matters A Working Class Anthology Of Prose Writing. Her poems have appeared online in Atrium, The Ofi Press, The Bangor Literary Journal, The Honest Ulsterman, HeadStuff, Dodging The Rain and many others.

Maeve was a recipient of two Arts Council of Ireland Awards, 2020/2021, a finalist in the Eavan Boland Mentorship Award, 2021 and a recipient of a John Hewitt Summer School bursary, 2021. She was placed third in the Canterbury Poet of The Year, 2021. Maeve was part of a poetry collaboration with three poets which won the Dreich Alliance Competition. This collection was published in Sept 2021.

About Fly on the Wall Press

A publisher with a conscience.
Publishing high quality anthologies, novels, short stories and poetry on pressing issues, from exceptional poets around the globe. Founded in 2018 by founding editor, Isabelle Kenyon.

Some other publications:

The Woman With An Owl Tattoo by Anne Walsh Donnelly
the sea refuses no river by Bethany Rivers
The Prettyboys of Gangster Town by Martin Grey
The Sound of the Earth Singing to Herself by Ricky Ray
Inherent by Lucia Orellana Damacela
Medusa Retold by Sarah Wallis
Pigskin by David Hartley
We Are All Somebody
Aftereffects by Jiye Lee
Someone Is Missing Me by Tina Tamsho-Thomas
Odd as F*ck by Anne Walsh Donnelly
Muscle and Mouth by Louise Finnigan
Modern Medicine by Lucy Hurst
These Mothers of Gods by Rachel Bower
Sin Is Due To Open In A Room Above Kitty's by Morag Anderson
Fauna by David Hartley
How To Bring Him Back by Clare HM
Hassan's Zoo and A Village in Winter by Ruth Brandt
No One Has Any Intention of Building A Wall by Ruth Brandt

Social Media:

@fly_press (Twitter) @flyonthewall_poetry (Instagram)
@flyonthewallpress (Facebook) www.flyonthewallpress.co.uk